I0605733

VALENTINE'S DAY BELLY LAUGHS & BITES

Anna Anderhagen

Consulting Editor, Diane Craig, MA/Reading Specialist

Super Sandcastle

An Imprint of Abdo Publishing
abdobooks.com

abdobooks.com

Published by Abdo Publishing, a division of ABDO, PO Box 398166, Minneapolis, Minnesota 55439.

Printed in the United States of America, North Mankato, Minnesota
102024
012025

Design: Layne Halvorsen, Mighty Media, Inc.
Production: Mighty Media, Inc.
Editor: Liz Salzmann
Cover Photographs: Mighty Media, Inc. (recipe photos); Shutterstock Images
Interior Photographs: Adobe Stock, pp. 9 (ice cream scoop, spoon), 10–11 (melting chocolate), 12 (hands), 13 (containers, washing plate), 20 (candy canes), 28–29 (child); Mighty Media, Inc. (recipe photos), pp. 10, 11, 14, 15, 16, 17, 18, 19, 20, 21, 22, 23, 24, 25, 26, 27, 29; Shutterstock Images, pp. 1 (rolling pin), 4–5 (old card), 5 (making card), 6 (all), 7 (child), 8 (blueberries, cereal, cherries, gummy fish, whipped cream), 8–9 (bottle), 9 (funnel, kettle, straws, sundae glass), 11 (food coloring, chocolate almond bark, toothpicks), 14 (cupid), 16 (bears), 18 (bottle), 22 (ladybugs), 26 (popcorn), 29 (plate, rolling pin), 30 (all), 31 (child)
Design Elements: Dedraw Studio/Shutterstock Images (abstract doodles), Lida Bu/Shutterstock Images (kitchen utensil doodles)

Library of Congress Control Number: 2024938365

Publisher's Cataloging-in-Publication Data
Names: Anderhagen, Anna, author.
Title: Valentine's day belly laughs & bites / by Anna Anderhagen
Description: Minneapolis, Minnesota : ABDO Publishing, 2025 | Series: Holiday jokes & sweet treats | Includes online resources and index.
Identifiers: ISBN 9781098295226 (lib. bdg.) | ISBN 9798384915270 (ebook)
Subjects: LCSH: Jokes--Juvenile literature. | Valentine's Day--Juvenile literature. | Holidays--Juvenile literature. | Snack foods--Juvenile literature. | Cooking--Juvenile literature. | Valentine's Day cookery--Juvenile literature.
Classification: DDC 398.7--dc23

TO ADULT HELPERS

The sweet treats in this series are fun and simple. There are just a few things to remember to keep kids safe. Creating some treats requires the use of hot objects. Also, kids may be using messy materials, such as food coloring. Make sure they protect their clothes and work surfaces. Review the projects before starting and be ready to assist when necessary.

Super Sandcastle™ books are created by a team of professional educators, reading specialists, and content developers around five essential components—phonemic awareness, phonics, vocabulary, text comprehension, and fluency—to assist young readers as they develop reading skills and strategies and increase their general knowledge. All books are written, reviewed, and leveled for guided reading and early reading intervention programs for use in shared, guided, and independent reading and writing activities to support a balanced approach to literacy instruction.

Contents

Valentine's Day 4
Holiday Hoots! 6
Sweet Materials 8
Almond Bark Tips & Tricks . . . 10
Treats Prep 12
Fruity Cupid's Arrows. 14
Bear Hug Pops. 16
Love Potion Floats. 18
Minty Valentines. 20
Lovey-Dovey Bugs 22
Popcorn Passion Mix 26
Keep Creating!. 28
Last Laughs. 30
Glossary. 32

VALENTINE'S DAY

Valentine's Day has a history that may go back to ancient Rome. The **Romans** had a **festival** called Lupercalia to **celebrate fertility**. It's possible that this festival led to the Christian **traditions** that developed later. The name "Valentine" comes from one or more Christian saints named Valentine who were honored on February 14.

Over time, Valentine's Day became more and more connected with love. In France and England, February 14 was thought to be when birds began mating. This led to the idea that the day should celebrate love and **romance**. Poets and authors began writing about love during this time.

In the United States, writing valentines began in the 1700s during the **American Revolution**. Soldiers and other people wrote love letters to their sweethearts. By 1900, people could buy mass-printed Valentine's Day cards. Today, more than one **billion** Valentine's Day cards are sent every year around the world!

Holiday Hoots!

What do you call a pig on February 14?

A Valen-swine.

What did one volcano say to the other on Valentine's Day?

I lava you.

What do you call a very small Valentine?

A valen-tiny.

What do you call two birds in love?

Tweet-hearts!

How do you keep a jewelry store safe on Valentine's Day?

You locket.

What did the tortoise say on Valentine's Day?

I turtle-ly love you.

What did the firefly eat at the Valentine's Day party?

A light snack!

What did one light bulb say to the other on Valentine's Day?

I love you a whole watt.

Sweet Materials

Here are some of the ingredients and tools you will need to make the treats in this book.

Ingredients

- baking soda
- blueberries
- brown chocolate candy
- butter
- candy eyes
- candy-coated chocolates
- canned whipped cream
- chocolate almond bark
- food coloring
- fruity ring-shaped cereal
- grenadine syrup
- lemon-lime soda
- light corn syrup
- maraschino cherries
- Milano cookies
- mini candy canes
- mini peanut butter cups
- mini vanilla wafers
- plain popped popcorn
- pretzel sticks
- rainbow sprinkles
- red candy strips
- red fruit leather
- red gummy fish
- red icing
- red licorice ropes
- red sprinkles or pearls
- strawberries
- sugar
- vanilla almond bark
- vanilla ice cream
- yogurt-covered pretzels

What did one piece of toast say to the other?

You're my butter half!

Tools

- aluminum foil
- baking pan
- baking sheet
- bowls
- condiment squeeze bottle
- curly straws
- funnel
- ice cream scoop
- kettle
- knife & cutting board
- lollipop sticks
- measuring cups & spoons
- microwave-safe bowl
- milkshake glasses
- parchment paper
- saucepan
- scissors
- skewers
- spoon

How do chefs show their love?

They whisk you off your feet!

Almond Bark Tips & Tricks

Some of the recipes in this book require chocolate or vanilla almond bark. Here are some tips for working with almond bark.

Tips for melting almond bark

- Cut the almond bark into small pieces. It will melt more quickly.
- Put the almond bark in a microwave-safe bowl.
- Microwave for 20 seconds at a time.
- Stir after each time. If you don't, the almond bark could burn.
- Repeat until the almond bark becomes creamy and smooth.
- Use oven mitts when you take it out of the microwave. The bowl will be hot!

What is a cow's favorite Valentine's Day dessert?

Chocolate moo-se

Tips for decorating with almond bark

- You can add food coloring to vanilla almond bark to make all sorts of colors!
- Melted almond bark is great for sticking things together and attaching decorations.
- When attaching small items, use a toothpick to put a little bit of melted almond bark on the items.

What did the drums say to the guitar on Valentine's Day?

My heart only beats for you.

Treats Prep

Be Safe

- Ask an adult for permission to use kitchen tools and ingredients.
- Ask an adult to help you use the microwave.
- Ask an adult for help when handling sharp or hot objects.
- Clean up spills right away.

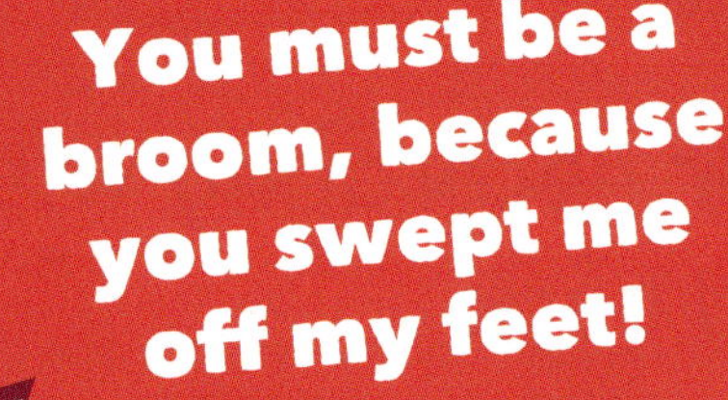

Get Ready!

- Wash your hands.
- Clean your work surface before you start.
- Read the list of tools and ingredients for the sweet treat you are making. Set out everything you will need.
- Read the whole recipe at least once before you start.

When You Are Finished

- Let hot treats cool completely.
- Put all the ingredients and tools away.
- Store leftover ingredients to use later.
- Wash all the dishes and cooking tools.
- Clean your work surface.
- Wash your hands before you eat your sweet treats!

Fruity Cupid's Arrows

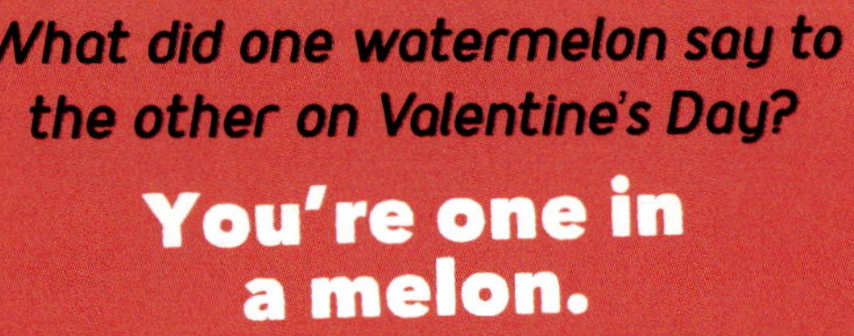

Ingredients

- 6 strawberries
- red gummy fish
- fruity ring-shaped cereal
- blueberries
- red candy strips

Tools

- knife & cutting board
- scissors
- 6 skewers

SWEET!

1. Cut the green tops off the strawberries. Cut each strawberry in half. Then cut the halves into heart shapes.
2. Cut 12 gummy fish into V shapes. Start at the tail and stop when you get to the head.
3. Stick the non-pointed end of a skewer into the top of a strawberry heart. This is the arrowhead.
4. Slide cereal and blueberries onto the skewer until it is almost covered.
5. When you get near the end of the skewer, add a folded piece of red candy strip.
6. Stick two of the fish onto the pointed end of the skewer. These are the arrow's feathers.

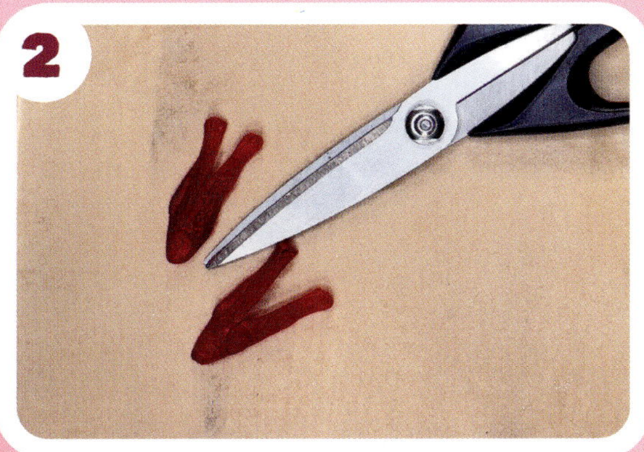

7. Repeat steps 3 through 6 to make more Fruity **Cupid's** Arrows to share with your friends.

Bear Hug Pops

What kind of socks do bears wear?

None. They have bare feet!

Ingredients

- 4 2-ounce squares of chocolate almond bark
- mini vanilla wafers
- mini peanut butter cups
- candy eyes
- brown chocolate candy
- rainbow sprinkles

Tools

- baking sheet
- parchment paper
- lollipop sticks
- knife & cutting board
- microwave-safe bowl
- spoon
- condiment squeeze bottle
- funnel

1. Line the baking sheet with parchment paper. Lay lollipop sticks on the baking sheet.
2. Follow the tips on page 10 to melt the almond bark. Use the funnel to pour it into the condiment bottle.
3. **Squeeze** a puddle of melted almond bark on one end of a lollipop stick.
4. Squeeze swirling lines of almond bark over and around the puddle for the bear's fur.
5. Add two vanilla wafers for the cheeks and two mini peanut butter cups for the ears.
6. Add two candy eyes and a chocolate candy nose. Add sprinkles over the whole head.
7. Repeat steps 3 through 6 to make more Bear Hug Pops.
8. Cool them in the refrigerator for 10 minutes. Serve to your friends and family for Valentine's Day!

What do you call a freezing bear?

A brrrrr!

Love Potion Floats

What did the rabbit say to his love on Valentine's Day?

Some-bunny loves you!

Ingredients

- 1 pint vanilla ice cream
- grenadine syrup
- 2-liter bottle of lemon-lime soda
- canned whipped cream
- red icing
- maraschino cherries

Tools

- ice cream scoop
- 2 milkshake glasses
- curly straws

1. Put two scoops of ice cream in each glass.
2. Add 2 quick pours of grenadine syrup to each glass.
3. Add lemon-lime soda until the glasses are three-fourths full.
4. Top them with whipped cream, red icing, and maraschino cherries.
5. Add straws and share the "love **potion**" with your secret crush!

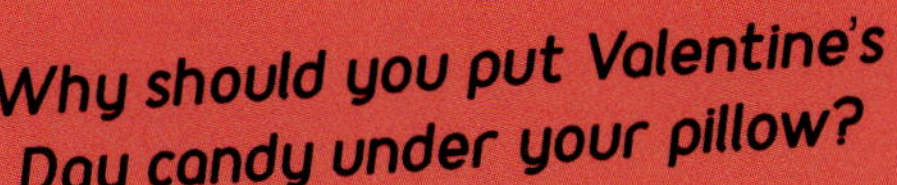

Why should you put Valentine's Day candy under your pillow?

It will give you sweet dreams!

2

3

4

Minty Valentines

What is a heart's favorite type of shoe?

Pumps!

Ingredients

* red fruit leather
* 12 mini candy canes
* 4 2-ounce squares of vanilla almond bark
* red or rainbow sprinkles or pearls

Tools

* scissors
* baking sheet
* parchment paper
* kettle
* bowl
* knife & cutting board
* microwave-safe bowl
* spoon

1. Cut the fruit leather into small squares. Fold each square in half and cut half of a heart along the folded edge. Unfold the hearts.
2. Line the baking sheet with parchment paper. Boil a kettle of water. Fill the bowl half full with hot water.
3. Carefully dip both ends of two candy canes in the hot water for 15 seconds.
4. Place the candy canes on the baking sheet. Press the tops and bottoms together to form a heart shape.

5. Repeat steps 3 and 4 to make more candy cane hearts. Let them cool for 10 minutes.

6. Follow the tips on page 10 to melt the almond bark.
7. Fill the candy cane hearts with melted almond bark. Gently press a fruit leather heart in the middle of each one. Add sprinkles.
8. Chill the Minty Valentines in the refrigerator for 15 minutes before serving.

Lovey-Dovey Bugs

When do bed bugs fall in love?
In the spring.

Ingredients

- red licorice ropes
- yogurt-covered pretzels
- Milano cookies
- vanilla almond bark
- red food coloring
- rainbow sprinkles
- candy eyes

Tools

- scissors
- baking sheet
- parchment paper
- knife & cutting board
- microwave-safe bowl
- spoon

ADORABLE!

1. Cut red licorice into strips a little longer than the cookies are wide. These will be the bugs' legs.
2. Break off two loops of some pretzels for the bugs' wings.
3. Line the baking sheet with parchment paper. Place cookies on the baking sheet.
4. Follow the tips on page 10 to melt the almond bark.

5. Stir three to five drops of red food coloring into the almond bark.

6. Spread melted almond bark on the cookies. Add rainbow sprinkles.

Continued on the next page.

7. Place two candy eyes at one end of each cookie. Place wings in the middle of each cookie.
8. Arrange three strips of licorice next to each other. Put some almond bark on the middle of the strips. Place a cookie on top so the legs stick out on each side.
9. Repeat step 8 to add legs to all of the cookie bugs.
10. Chill the cookies in the refrigerator for 10 minutes. Then serve to your friends for Valentine's Day!

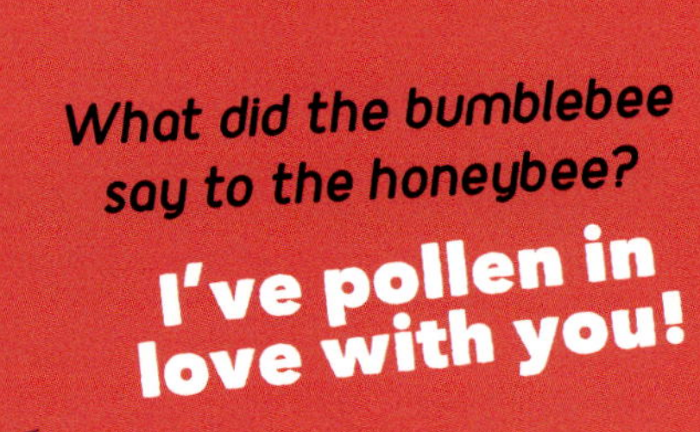

YUM!

What did the love bug say to the bee?

You are so buzz-arre!

Popcorn Passion Mix

What did the painter say to her sweetheart?

I love you with all my art!

Ingredients

- about 30 pretzel sticks
- 10 cups plain popped popcorn
- 1 cup sugar
- ½ cup (1 stick) butter
- ¼ cup light corn syrup
- red food coloring
- ¾ teaspoon baking soda
- candy-coated chocolates

Tools

- measuring cups & spoons
- large bowl
- saucepan
- spoon
- baking pan
- aluminum foil

WOW!

1. Preheat the oven to 200 degrees Fahrenheit (93°C). Break the pretzels into small pieces. Put them and the popcorn in a large bowl.
2. Put the sugar, butter, and corn syrup in a saucepan. Bring to a boil on medium heat.
3. Stir in ten drops of red food coloring and the baking soda. The mixture will foam up a bit.
4. Remove from heat. Pour the mixture over the popcorn and pretzels. Toss to coat evenly.
5. Line the baking pan with foil. Spread the popcorn evenly on the baking pan.

6. Bake for 1 hour, stirring every 15 minutes. Cool completely. Stir in candy-coated chocolates. Serve Popcorn Passion Mix to your friends!

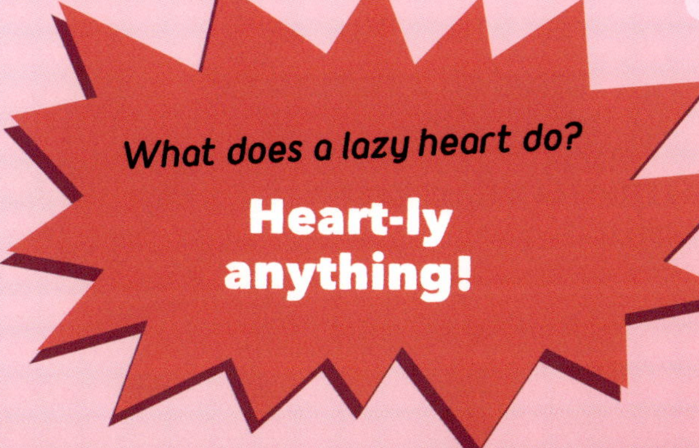

Keep Creating!

You've made some **delicious** treats with the recipes in this book! Hopefully you had some laughs with your friends too. But could you make any of the recipes differently? Or can you think of your own Valentine's Day treat?

Do you or a friend have a nut **allergy**? Try making the Bear Hug Pops with chocolate-covered caramels instead of mini peanut butter cups for the ears.

Does a treat include an ingredient you don't like? Get creative! Find something else to use that you do like. For example, you could add mini marshmallows to your Fruity **Cupid's** Arrows instead of blueberries. You could melt white chocolate chips instead of vanilla almond bark for the Lovey-Dovey Bugs or Minty Valentines.

How did the almond share its feelings with the peanut?

It said, "I'm nuts about you!"

Just use your imagination to keep creating!

Last Laughs

What did the flame say when he met the love of his life?

I found the perfect match!

Where did the spaghetti take its sweetheart on Valentine's Day?

To the meat-ball!

What do elephants say to each other on Valentine's Day?

I love you a ton.

What do you call someone who draws hearts?

A heart-ist!

What did the snail write in its Valentine's Day card?
Be my Valen-slime.
What did one oar say to the other?
I love our row-mance.
What do you call someone who has a cold on Valentine's Day?
Lovesick.
What did one sheep say to the other on February 14?
I love ewe!

Glossary

allergy – a sickness caused by touching, breathing, or eating certain things.

American Revolution – the war between Americans and the British from 1775 to 1783. The Americans won their freedom from the British.

billion – a very large number. One billion is also written 1,000,000,000.

celebrate – to observe a holiday with special events.

cupid – a fictional baby with wings holding a bow and arrow that is based on the Roman god of love.

delicious – very pleasing to taste.

fertility – the ability to have children.

festival – a celebration that often happens at the same time each year.

potion – liquids mixed together to make a medicine or poison.

romance – the feeling between two people who are in love.

Romans – the people who lived in ancient Rome from about 27 BCE to 476 CE.

squeeze – to press the sides of something together.

tradition – a belief or practice passed through a family or group of people.